# ANDREW CARNEGIE'S PEACE ENDOWMENT

## The Nineteen-Eighties

Carnegie Endowment for International Peace
Washington, D.C.
1985

ISBN 0-87003-041-8
Library of Congress Catalog Number: 85-62058
Printed in the United States of America

# *Foreword*

During 1985-86, the Carnegie Endowment for International Peace celebrates the Diamond Jubilee of its creation by Andrew Carnegie in 1910 as the first major American foundation devoted to research and public education on world affairs.

Over this three-quarters of a century, the Endowment has changed, of course, as the times have changed. It has shifted its focus and methods, as its founder intended. While remaining a private institution which has never accepted government funds, the Endowment has in recent decades been an operating foundation, not a grant-making one. Today its professional core of Senior Associates and Resident Associates—approximately twenty at any one time—are normally appointed for a year or two to write about some significant international issue with which they have had recent and intense personal involvement. Diplomats and other officials, academics and journalists—Americans and non-Americans alike—come to the Endowment prepared to write for professional journals and the public press. The Endowment, for its part, tries to provide a congenial atmosphere for them to do so.

*Thomas L. Hughes, president*

Originally founded in Washington, during the last five years the Endowment has fully returned to its 1910 place of origin. At various periods in its history, it also had substantial offices in Paris (1912-54), Geneva (1954-78), and New York (1910-83). Over the years, changing patterns of operation, fluctuations in exchange rates, and economies of scale combined to argue for consolidation in one place. Since the closing of the Endowment's New York office in Rockefeller Center in 1983, this has meant a concentration of resources at Dupont Circle in Washington.

Curiously, perhaps fortuitously, consolidation in Washington coincided with the years when Washington itself was experiencing a tremendous unleashing of non-governmental foreign affairs analysis. Once alone in the world of 1910 in its mission of producing policy-relevant international affairs research, the Endowment now finds itself but one element in a mushrooming industry of think tanks, special-interest groups, and ideological shrines. Such a hot-house environment invites introspection about identity and differentiation, about purposes and methods.

Like other serious research organizations, we are up against, and have to live with, some pervasive and ominous new tendencies:

- the predicament of information saturation—too much writing, too many sources, too many conduits;

- the force-feeding of the over-informed, with quality at the mercy of quantity, and the highest possible level of confusion the frequent result;

- the struggle for attention and preferment between the 2,000 or so foreign-policy analysts inside the Washington Beltway, and the say 200,000 or 2,000,000 outside;

- the recent growth of ideological litmus tests designed to channel friendly analysis to strategically-placed recipients;

- the gratuitous pigeon-holing and artificial labeling of individuals and institutions by the adversary-oriented media;

- the special handicaps confronting objective analysis of international politics, as the gap between world trends and official U.S. policies grows ever wider, with consequences for East-West, West-West, and North-South relations alike; and

- the consequent tendency for pluralism to give way to polarization, as ideological adversaries break into affinity clusters—roving packs that unnecessarily widen existing cleavages and polemicize the nation's higher politics.

In Ronald Reagan's Washington, the research agenda is now being shaped by particular groups with a particular stake in a particular outcome supportive of the president's policies. The landscape of the capital city is littered with war games and war-related scenarios set by the new ideological influentials, their finances abun-

dant because many in corporate America are willing to invest in predictable research, the best that money can buy.

Named in 1910 when "peace" was establishmentarian and non-controversial, the Carnegie Endowment now operates in an environment where "peace" is officially suspect. It carries this semantic handicap, confident that this, too, will change. In the meantime, the Endowment engages the central war/peace issues of the day not as a group of "peace activists" or as a "peace lobby," but as a generator and broker of ideas that serious people can take seriously. The Endowment does not believe that peace is self-defining or likely to emerge from the streets; it does believe that peace has something important to do with a principled and enlightened internationalism in American foreign policy.

Over the generations, internationalism of one form or another was intuitive for the Carnegie Endowment's leadership, from Elihu Root and Nicholas Murray Butler in the early days, through John Foster Dulles and Dwight D. Eisenhower in the 1940s and 1950s, to their less orthodox successor trustees of the 1960s, 1970s, and 1980s. By contrast, internationalism has today become counter-intuitive for America's ascendant official leadership, and often for its ascendant official opposition as well, a development that is bound to condition the context in which the Endowment operates. New Right Republicans and New Politics Democrats have become the new establishments of the two politi-

*Larry L. Fabian, secretary*

cal parties, artificially polarizing the scene even more.

This constitutes a reversal of textbook normality. Instead of the compromisers being inside the government, putting together cross-cutting coalitions, the executive branch and its opposition seem increasingly captured by irreconcilables. In a sense, non-governmental institutions have inherited the mediating role left over from previous governments and the old parties. Predictable people inhabit many government and party posts, while the bridge builders and searchers for common ground operate on the outside.

As the Endowment's Guidelines (see page 70) demonstrate, this organization is among those that remain committed to pluralism in the discourse on world affairs and opposed to the rampant polarization. We are quite ready to hire and defend individuals who have the courage of their convictions and who express themselves strongly on combustible issues. They speak for themselves, not for the Endowment; that is their preference, and it is ours.

As an institution, we desire to engage, not in Official Research and not in Oppositionist Research, but in open research—not "research on command" or result-driven, politically-skewed research, but untrammeled research.

In shunning ideology, the Endowment continues to pay tribute to the unalterable complexities of world affairs, to the sober understanding of international realities, rather than to the fashionable make-believe world of the true believers and the hot-eyed zealots, whoever they may be, wherever they may live, and whatever nations they may temporarily govern.

The Endowment marks this anniversary year with three special publications. *Estrangement: America and the World,* coming from Oxford University Press, is a collection of provocative essays examining the position of the United States in the postwar period. *Andrew Carnegie's Peace Endowment: The Tycoon, the President, and Their Bargain of 1910* is the fascinating story of the Endowment's origins, much of it previously untold and now admirably recounted by Larry Fabian in a richly illustrated booklet that is available on request.

Here, in the third publication, we thought the most vivid way to present the recent life of the Endowment would be to recapitulate in text and pictures the great variety of topics and of people who have worked here during the past five years. As the text makes clear, the larger life of the Endowment is greatly enriched by outreach programs like the Face-to-Face discussions; the Endowment's quarterly magazine, *Foreign Policy;* and the manifold activities of the Arms Control Association. The Endowment's support staff, capably managed by Michael O'Hare, as well as its regular stream of visiting interns, are indispensable to the smooth running of the organization. So too, of course, is the ever-efficient and accommodating Carnegie Endowment Library, under the insightful management of Librarian Jane Lowenthal.

Joint sponsorship of occasional meetings with other organizations is another form of Endowment outreach. An example is the monthly Mid-Atlantic Club luncheon, co-sponsored by the Endowment and the office of the European Communities in Washington. Guest presentations on U.S.-European issues provide a forum for discussion among private experts, former officials, interested academics and journalists, and current representatives of U.S. and European governmental, financial, economic, and social organizations.

The Endowment also continues to benefit from its co-location with other institutions of such congenial and overlapping interests as the Washington office of the Council on Foreign Relations, under the leadership of Alton Frye; the grant-making German Marshall Fund of the United States, led by Frank Loy; and the Institute for International Economics, headed by Fred Bergsten. The latter two were at one time infant organizations, administratively incubated by the Endowment until they were fully funded and staffed. That nurturing is another kind of public service the Endowment has been proud to render over the years. We are pleased that the En-

*John W. Douglas, chairman of the Board of Trustees*

dowment's Conference Center has become a favorite Washington environment for deliberations and debate sponsored by a wide variety of public-policy organizations.

Overall responsibility for this and other Endowment anniversary publications belongs to Sanford J. Ungar, well-known author, editor, and commentator, who has been ably assisted here by David Weiner. The photographs of Endowment trustees and staff are the sensitive and highly skilled work of Chad Evans Wyatt.

The diversity we have tried to maintain will be evident in the following pages. The pluralism is assured by short-term appointments, regular turnover of most appointees, the great variety of governmental experience in various administrations, the presence of non-Americans on the staff, and the fact that associates at the Endowment are not beholden to any interested business, party, or individual for their appointment or their sustenance. All of them are, in the best sense, free to write in the public interest, not the funder's interest. That has been the Endowment's practice for seventy-five years, and it remains our practice today.

*Thomas L. Hughes, President*
*Carnegie Endowment*
*August 1985*

*I*n recent years the Endowment's work on issues of international security and arms control has been complemented by its work in Soviet-American relations. Just as the arms control process and the debate over defense strategy have been profoundly affected by the uncertain status of relations between the superpowers, so the overall quality of these relations is conditioned by perceptions of the strategic balance and the rate of progress toward arms control. Several projects combined research on key aspects of arms control with related geopolitical issues. Specialists in American, European

Leslie H. Gelb

## Carnegie Panel on U.S. Security and the Future of Arms Control

| | |
|---|---|
| William Beecher | Jan M. Lodal |
| Seweryn Bialer | William D. Nordhaus |
| Sydney M. Cone, III | Joseph S. Nye, Jr. |
| John Deutch | Philip A. Odeen |
| Capt. Joseph A. Engelbrecht, Jr. | Lt. Gen. Robert E. Pursley (ret.) |
| Gregory C. Farrington | Lt. Gen. Brent Scowcroft (ret.) |
| Richard L. Garwin | Lt. Col. Michael B. Seaton |
| Leslie H. Gelb | Walter Slocombe |
| Gen. Andrew Goodpaster (ret.) | Leon Sloss |
| Vice Adm. Patrick J. Hannifin (ret.) | Stephen Stamas |
| Stanley Hoffmann | Richard C. Steadman |
| Thomas L. Hughes | Robert B. Stobaugh |
| William G. Hyland | Strobe Talbott |
| Eli Jacobs | Richard H. Ullman |
| Edward G. Jordan | Maj. Thomas R. Wheelock |
| Tom Kahn | R. James Woolsey, Jr. |
| Nicola Khuri | Maj. Edward Wright |
| Franklin A. Lindsay | |

and Soviet foreign policy have at the same time undertaken studies of military strategy and weapons negotiations.

In 1980 the Endowment established a Panel on U.S. Security and the Future of Arms Control. Its work was directed toward narrowing the range of responsible argument over arms control by identifying a common denominator of agreed facts and realities. Under the chairmanship of Carnegie Associate Leslie H. Gelb, former director of the State Department's Bureau of Politico-Military Affairs, the panel brought together a distinguished, bipartisan group of arms control and security specialists, scientists, journalists, business people, attorneys, and military officials. Meeting twice monthly in working groups or in full sessions, the panel produced four influential reports.

In its first major undertaking, the panel explored the relationship between defense spending and the performance of the U.S. economy and it broadly assessed the U.S.-Soviet strategic balance. The second report compared the conventional military forces and levels of defense spending of the United States and the Soviet Union. The third report evaluated the deterrent value and the command and control of American strategic forces. It was completed under the cochairmanship of Carnegie Associate William G. Hyland, former deputy national security adviser to President Gerald Ford, and Joseph S. Nye, Jr., professor of government at Harvard University. A final report examined arms treaty verification, Soviet negotiating behavior, the arms limitation implications of certain fundamental problems in nuclear strategy, and the problems and prospects of major arms control approaches that had been proposed in the early 1980s.

The publication of each of the panel's reports was accompanied by an extensive public outreach program. Reporters and editors attended formal press conferences in Washington and New York, and de-

*Marshall D. Shulman, director of the Harriman Institute for Advanced Study of the Soviet Union at Columbia University, is introduced by John W. Douglas before speaking to Carnegie trustees and associates*

tailed briefing sessions were conducted for specialists. The panel generated substantial editorial comment in major newspapers and magazines throughout the United States and abroad.

While chairing the Future of Arms Control Panel, Gelb pursued his own research and writing on arms control and related issues. In an article published in *Foreign Policy,* he argued that the ambitious arms control process of the 1970s had, in large measure, failed, and he called for an alternative, more incremental approach. In a later *Foreign Policy* piece, Gelb and Richard H. Ullman, then editor of the magazine, examined American policy in the

aftermath of the Soviet invasion of Afghanistan. Gelb's study of the impact on American foreign policy of the rivalry between the State Department and the National Security Council led to essays in the *Washington Quarterly* and the *New York Times Magazine.* Before assuming the post of national security correspondent for the *New York Times,* he wrote several other articles on arms control, U.S. defense policy, and Soviet-American relations.

Upon completing his service as U.S. representative to the NATO-Warsaw Pact Mutual and Balanced Force Reduction (MBFR) talks in Vienna, Ambassador Jonathan Dean joined the Endowment, bring-

*Jonathan Dean*

An official statement by the government of France that, in the event of Soviet attack, French forces would come to the support of NATO forces would of itself do a great deal to invigorate NATO conventional defense.

Jonathan Dean,
*Foreign Policy,*
Fall 1982.

*Trustees William J. Perry and Barbara W. Newell*

ing his experience to bear on a range of arms reduction and national security issues. In an article that received widespread attention, Dean argued that an improvement of NATO's defenses could be undertaken simultaneously with an effort to reach a conventional arms reduction agreement with the Warsaw Pact in Europe. He thus lent his voice to a small but influential group of former U.S. and European officials who succeeded in initiating a major policy debate over NATO strategy in the early 1980s.

Writing in other journals and newspapers, and speaking before groups of concerned citizens and specialists, Dean brought greater attention to the MBFR talks, the least well-known of the major arms control efforts. At the conclusion of his Carnegie project in 1984, he became the senior arms control specialist at the Union of Concerned Scientists.

The Carnegie Endowment's arms control verification project was headed by Michael Krepon, former director of defense program and policy reviews at the U.S. Arms Control and Disarmament Agency, and underwritten in part by the Ploughshares Fund. Krepon's objective was to develop policy recommendations for the adequate policing of arms treaty provisions and formal procedures for resolving compliance conflicts. He assembled a group of experts who met on a regular basis to discuss these issues.

Krepon also sought to reach beyond the project's professional constituency to encourage public discussion of these increasingly politicized topics. He replied to frequent media inquiries and addressed verification matters in diverse publications, including his pamphlet *Arms Control: Verification and Compliance* for the Headline Series of the Foreign Policy Association. Late in 1984, St. Martin's Press published Krepon's study of the American arms control debate, *Strategic Stalemate: Nuclear Weapons and Arms Control in*

*Michael Krepon, second from left, addresses a luncheon organized by the Endowment's interns. Second from right is Marie M. Hoguet, education coordinator of the Arms Control Association*

The last time the United States was surprised by a new Soviet program with strategic significance was when Sputnik, the U.S.S.R.'s first satellite, was launched in 1957.

Michael Krepon,
*Arms Control: Verification and Compliance*, 1984.

American Politics, which he wrote while an International Affairs Fellow of the Council on Foreign Relations, prior to coming to the Endowment.

By the beginning of the 1980s, efforts to stem the proliferation of nuclear arms no longer commanded the high priority on the international agenda that they had previously enjoyed. The Endowment's nuclear nonproliferation project, underwritten by the Carnegie Corporation and the Rockefeller Brothers Fund, was launched by Leonard S. Spector, former chief counsel of the U.S. Senate Subcommittee on Energy and Nuclear Proliferation. The project has sought to increase awareness of the urgency of this issue by preparing an annual, book-length study entitled *Nuclear Proliferation Today.* In 1984, the first volume was published in hardcover by Ballinger and in paperback by Vintage Books.

On a country-by-country basis, the reports evaluate developments during the previous year that have served to retard or to promote the spread of nuclear weaponry. They have also highlighted the activities of nuclear suppliers and regulatory bodies like the International Atomic Energy Agency. Appendices containing chronologies and primers on nuclear technology and nonproliferation concepts

*Leonard S. Spector, foreground, at a* Foreign Policy *press breakfast introducing the first volume of* Nuclear Proliferation Today

Valuable as the international non-proliferation regime has been in slowing the spread of nuclear arms, it has not succeeded in halting the process, and the trend toward further proliferation is continuing.

Leonard S. Spector,
*Nuclear Proliferation Today,* 1984.

*Rudolph C. Noble, of the Endowment's Finance and Administration department*

*William G. Hyland*

have made these reports useful for the general public as well as specialists.

William Hyland came to the Endowment after a distinguished governmental career dealing with national security issues. While at Carnegie, he worked particularly on problems in Soviet-American relations, including the Soviet invasion of Afghanistan in 1979, the deployment of new NATO missiles in Western Europe, the collapse of nuclear arms reduction talks in 1983, and the shooting down of Korean Airlines flight 007 that same year. He also explored the Soviet succession process and the nascent accommodation between the Soviet Union and the People's Republic of China, two issues that complicated efforts to resolve the array of conflicts besetting U.S.-Soviet relations in the 1980s.

In an article for the journal *Problems of Communism,* Hyland weighed the prospects for significant change in Soviet policy under the successors to President Leonid Brezhnev. Hyland's views on this question also appeared in the *New Republic, Foreign Policy* and other publications, and in testimony before Congress. His interest in the shifting Sino-Soviet relationship led to a collection of essays, *The China Factor,* which he edited for the American Assembly.

> **T**he administration needs to shed the neoisolationist tendencies of conservative Republicans and recognize that the superpower struggle is for the heart and mind of Western Europe.
>
> William G. Hyland,
> *Foreign Policy,*
> Winter 1982-83.

*Carnegie Trustees Marjorie Craig Benton, George N. Lindsay, Robert F. Goheen, Hedley Donovan, and Richard A. Debs*

Hyland also participated in several major symposiums on Soviet-American relations, including the Dartmouth Group of American public and private citizens who have been meeting informally with Soviet officials for more than a decade. In 1984 he left the Endowment to assume the editorship of *Foreign Affairs.*

Dimitri K. Simes focused on the Soviet end of the superpower relationship. A former research associate at the Institute of World Economy and International Relations in Moscow, Simes established himself as a recognized authority on Soviet affairs and U.S.-Soviet relations. During his tenure at the Endowment, his opinions on current and emerging developments—in particular, on the Soviet Union's three leadership changes during the early 1980s—were often sought by members of the press and the policy community.

Simes's commentaries were regularly featured in the *Christian Science Monitor* and also appeared frequently on the op-ed pages of the *New York Times* and other newspapers. His major writing projects included a two-part essay on Soviet policies and alternative American responses published in *Foreign Policy* in 1984. Simes was frequently interviewed on major national television and radio news programs.

While serving as executive director of

*Dimitri K. Simes*

**M**aintaining military and geopolitical pressure on the Soviet Union is not an obstacle to a more constructive and stable relationship. On the contrary, it may be a condition for a thaw.

Dimitri K. Simes,
*New York Times,*
April 19, 1985.

the Arms Control Association (ACA) from 1977-1984, William H. Kincade was also a Carnegie associate. In his diverse writings, addresses, and research collaborations, Kincade made important contributions to arms control analysis and national security education. He regularly wrote articles for essay collections, journals, and newspapers in the United States and abroad, co-edited three books, and prepared the script for a British Broadcasting Corporation television documentary on military technology and arms control, which he hosted. Kincade also collaborated with Dr. Stephen Sonnenberg of the Washington School of Psychiatry on the principal working paper for a 1984 conference on the psychology of nuclear deterrence, co-sponsored by the Carnegie Endowment and the school. A revised and expanded version of this paper was scheduled to be published in 1986 by Yale University Press.

In 1984 the Ford Foundation backed an ambitious education project, entitled National Security in the Nuclear Age, which emerged from the curriculum development and instructional programs on which ACA, at Kincade's initiative, had collaborated with the Consortium on International Studies Education during the early 1980s. Sponsored by the Mershon Center of Ohio State University, this multiyear endeavor sought to develop classroom materials, curricula, and teaching skills for the purpose of introducing national security issues into secondary school classrooms. After leaving ACA, Kincade continued to serve as one of the project's directors while pursuing his own writing on technology and national security at the Endowment.

The revolution in military hardware since World War II has radically transformed the capabilities, political functions, and costs of military power. Under the direction of Barry M. Blechman, former assistant director of the U.S. Arms Control and Disarmament Agency, one

> **I**f human ingenuity can design an effective ballistic missile defense, human ingenuity also can develop the means to penetrate it.
>
> William H. Kincade,
> *Chicago Tribune,*
> January 20, 1985.

*William H. Kincade, left, and Barry M. Blechman*

Endowment project sought to examine the novel means and mechanisms by which military power—short of the actual outbreak of hostilities—influences contemporary international politics.

Blechman first explored the relationship between nuclear weapons and foreign policy, attempting to explain how changes in the strategic nuclear balance affect the basic character of relations among the major nuclear powers and their allies. He then investigated the political consequences of developments in conventional military technology. His essay on the utility of military power in Third World conflicts was published as an *Adelphi Paper* by the International Institute for Strategic Studies in London. In other articles Blechman evaluated the U.S. defense budget debate and the U.S.-Soviet negotiation effort between 1977 and 1979 to limit conventional arms transfers to the Third World. After leaving Carnegie, he became a senior fellow at Georgetown University's Center for Strategic and International Studies and later started his own defense consulting firm.

Richard Burt, national security correspondent for the *New York Times,* joined the Endowment for a period, writing on U.S.-Soviet relations and arms control. His essay "The Relevance of Arms Control in the 1980s" appeared in an issue of *Daedalus,* the journal of the American Academy of Arts and Sciences, devoted to an overview of key challenges facing U.S. defense policy in the 1980s. The project was funded by the Ford and Scaife foundations. The Endowment arranged and hosted the preparatory authors' and editorial conferences in which Burt, as well as several other members of the Carnegie staff, participated. The essays were subsequently published in hardcover by Little, Brown and Company. Soon after he returned to the *Times,* Burt was appointed director of the State Department's Bureau of Politico-Military Affairs in the Reagan administration.

*Trustee William B. Macomber, above, and, far right, former Vice Chairman of the Board John Chancellor with Trustee Charles W. Bailey II and Sanford J. Ungar*

The demise of U.S.-Soviet détente and significant ideological shifts in several Western governments beginning in the late 1970s brought European issues to the fore of international concerns once again during the early 1980s. Controversies surrounding the neutron bomb, the deployment of intermediate-range missiles in Western Europe, the antinuclear movement, neutralist sentiments, international economic friction, and the collapse of arms control talks in 1983 all took a significant toll on relations in the alliance.

James O. Goldsborough's book *Rebel Europe,* published by Macmillan, offered a comprehensive, provocative assessment of some of the broad changes that were taking place within Europe and in Europe's relations with the superpowers during the early 1980s. Goldsborough, former Paris bureau chief for *Newsweek,* surveyed the political and economic evolution of Western Europe and the resulting frictions with the United States. In particular, he focused on the emergence of a consensus in West European capitals on the necessity of developing an autonomous relationship that would permit them to follow a more independent course in areas not directly related to NATO interests.

The Soviets faced parallel difficulties in Eastern Europe, Goldsborough asserted, because the creation of links between Eastern and Western Europe had served to constrain Soviet action in the former. He identified a fundamental dilemma facing Moscow in the 1980s: An improvement in relations between the two halves of Europe could only be achieved at the cost of increasing Eastern Europe's political exposure; yet the alternative to liberalization was the maintenance of a hermetic purity that would return Eastern Europe to the more financially burdensome and politically tense isolation it knew during the cold war. After leaving the Endow-

*Clockwise, Charles J. Zwick, Vice Chairman of the Board; Trustees James C. Gaither, George C. Lodge, and Norman F. Ramsey*

ment, Goldsborough went on to become associate editor of the *San Jose Mercury-News* in California.

In his project on European-American relations, Josef Joffe, former senior editor of the German weekly *Die Zeit,* analyzed the gradual improvement in relations between the United States and Western Europe from the early to the mid-1980s. Recognizing the potential costs of a major rupture, Joffe noted, Europeans and Americans had begun to display greater sensitivity toward each other.

Joffe's surveys of the state of transatlantic relations appeared in year-end issues of *Foreign Affairs* and the *Naval War College Review.* In an article for the Spring 1984 issue of *Foreign Policy*, he assessed various proposals to deal with the alleged weakness of NATO's conventional defenses. Joffe's commentaries on current topics ran in numerous newspapers in the United States and Europe. At the conclusion of his project, he assumed the post of foreign editor of the *Süddeutsche Zeitung.*

Gebhard L. Schweigler, a specialist on U.S.-European relations at the *Stiftung Wissenschaft und Politik* near Munich, was at the Endowment during 1984-1985. His work was aimed primarily at evaluating the domestic underpinnings of relations between the United States and Western Europe. Schweigler conveyed his impressions of U.S. attitudes in articles and essays for a range of West German books and journals. In these, and in features broadcast by Bavarian Radio, he took up the so-called Europeanization of America, American foreign policy, and U.S. relations with Germany and the Soviet Union.

The domestic setting of West German foreign policy was the subject of Schweigler's *Washington Paper* monograph for the Georgetown University Center for Strategic and International Studies, which was translated and published in Germany in 1985. He also wrote essays on relations between East and West Germany

*Gebhard L. Schweigler*

and on anti-Americanism in West Germany for several publications in the United States. Before returning to Munich, Schweigler had the opportunity to discuss these questions with university and research institute audiences, seeking especially to counter the prevailing—and, in his view, erroneous—perception of increasing American disinterest in Europe.

Leaving his post as director of the State Department's Office of Soviet Affairs, Robert K. German joined the Endowment to investigate Nordic-Soviet relations. In two widely discussed essays, for the journals *Orbis* and *International Security,* he addressed Soviet efforts to weaken Scandi-

navia's—and especially Norway's—ties with the West. German analyzed Moscow's encouragement of the Norwegian peace movement and the Soviet attempt to exploit the restrictions that Norway has traditionally imposed upon its own defense activities. Although he believed the chances that the Norwegians might withdraw from NATO were slim, he warned that damaging alliance tensions would grow unless Soviet pressures were effectively opposed. After leaving Carnegie, German became dean of the School of Area Studies in the State Department's Foreign Service Institute. In 1985 he was appointed distinguished visiting Tom

Slick professor of world peace at the LBJ School of Public Affairs of the University of Texas.

John Di Sciullo, a retired U.S. Foreign Service officer with many years of experience in Italy, came to the Endowment to write about changes in Italian politics. Prior to the 1983 Italian parliamentary election, in which the Socialist party for the first time obtained the premiership for its leader, Di Sciullo reviewed the volatile Italian political situation at conferences and in commentaries for the American and Italian media. In the election's aftermath, he assessed its implications for Italy's long-standing policies toward the

*Robert K. German*

United States and the NATO alliance. Using his extensive contacts among Italian politicians, journalists, and scholars, Di Sciullo organized and participated in several meetings on U.S.-Italian relations.

Upon leaving the State Department, where he had been senior European specialist in the Office of Long-Range Assessment and Research, Eric Willenz arrived at Carnegie in 1985. He attempted to illuminate the foreign-policy consequences of the effort by conservative governments in Western Europe, with U.S. encouragement, to dismantle some of the central components of the European welfare state. In the course of his research, Wil-

lenz examined the historical role of welfare states in the development of European democracy and their contribution to social stability.

Warren Zimmermann, who had just completed an assignment as deputy chief of mission at the U.S. embassy in Moscow, came to the Endowment as an international affairs fellow of the Council on Foreign Relations, focusing on the political future of Europe. Several months later, Zimmermann was appointed deputy to Max Kampelman, head of the Reagan administration's delegation to the U.S.-Soviet arms negotiations that resumed in Geneva in the spring of 1985.

Michael H. C. McDowell, a journalist from Northern Ireland, spent a year at the Endowment exploring the political conflict there, its roots in centuries of religious tension between Protestants and Roman Catholics, and the complications of present-day Irish nationalism. McDowell attempted especially to raise American consciousness of the causes, dangerous consequences, and possible solutions to this seemingly intractable conflict. In frequent articles, especially for newspapers published in cities with sizable Irish-American populations and for national Catholic publications, McDowell described the Protestant-majority communi-

*Warren Zimmermann*

*Eric Willenz*

ty in Northern Ireland, where he had been raised. He also considered the roles of the British and Irish republican governments in the Ulster issue, the effects of segregated education, and the political initiatives of leading Irish-American politicians. McDowell later joined the Canadian Broadcasting Corporation, becoming a producer of one of its current affairs radio programs.

James W. Spain, whose American diplomatic career has included six years' service in Turkey—two of these as ambassador—devoted part of his time at the Endowment to the question of Turkey's role in the Western alliance. In a *Foreign Policy* article coauthored with Carnegie Associate Nicholas S. Ludington, Spain examined the process by which the military regime of Kenan Evren returned Turkey to democratic rule.

Spain also undertook an evaluation of the role of U.S. ambassadors and missions abroad in the implementation of American foreign policy. In articles for *Worldview* and the *Foreign Service Journal,* and in numerous public appearances, he challenged the widespread impression that ambassadors are irrelevant to the execution of U.S. foreign policy in an age of rapid communication, diplomatic summits, and special envoys. Spain was named U.S. ambassador to Sri Lanka in 1985, after a period as a senior analyst with the Rand Corporation.

Ludington, former Middle East bureau chief of the Associated Press, looked into the foreign implications of internal political developments in Turkey. The article he wrote with Spain generated panel dis-

James W. Spain

Seldom in recent years has a secretary of state's first thought in a crisis been, "What does our ambassador think?"

James W. Spain,
*Washington Quarterly,*
Spring 1983.

cussions cosponsored by the Endowment and the Middle East Institute. In other writings, for the *Los Angeles Times* and the *Boston Globe,* Ludington considered the charged issue of Armenian nationalism and the 1983 pre-election scenario in Turkey. The constitutional process was the subject of his addresses before university and business audiences. At the conclusion of his Endowment project, Ludington became United Nations correspondent for the Associated Press.

Jane E. Lowenthal,
Endowment librarian

By contrast to Poland, East Germany is a miracle of political stability. Its internal peace rests not so much on Soviet bayonets (of which there are 400,000 in the country) as on West German generosity that spells free trade, technology transfers and economic subsidies.

Josef Joffe,
*Los Angeles Times,*
August 16, 1984.

*T*he most significant developments in the Middle East during the early 1980s—the rise of Islamic fundamentalism, the crisis in Lebanon, and the stalemate in the Arab-Israeli peace process—were the subject of several Endowment projects.

Ze'ev Schiff, Israel's most respected defense journalist and coeditor with Larry Fabian of *Israelis Speak,* published in 1977, joined the Endowment in 1983 to study Israeli security policy. Following up on the work begun in his controversial Israeli bestseller *Israel's Lebanon War* (published in English by Simon and Schuster in 1984), Schiff, chief military af-

**R**esentment against the West is probably more widespread in the Moslem world as a whole than anti-Sovietism, because up to now more Moslem countries have had direct experience of Western imperialism than of the Soviet variety.

Edward Mortimer,
*Faith and Power: The
Politics of Islam,* 1982.

*Ze'ev Schiff*

fairs editor for the newspaper *Ha'aretz,* explored the international consequences and domestic repercussions of Israel's 1982 invasion and occupation of Lebanon.

Schiff also addressed the precarious balance of competing political and military forces in Lebanon, the Lebanese conflict's psychological and political consequences in Israel, and the new challenges facing U.S. Middle East policy in the aftermath of the invasion. To all of these endeavors he brought a unique understanding of Israel's armed forces. His special perspective on Israeli affairs and the Lebanon war made him a frequent subject of radio and television interviews for media in Canada, Europe, Israel, and the United States. Schiff returned to *Ha'aretz* in 1985.

The far-reaching revival of Islamic fundamentalism during the late 1970s, manifested most powerfully in the 1979 Iranian revolution, largely took the West by surprise. Motivated by the desire to make these developments more comprehensible to Western readers, Edward Mortimer, an editorial writer for the *Times* of London with many years of experience reporting on the Middle East, came to the Endowment to work on his highly regarded book *Faith and Power: The Politics of Islam,* published in 1982 by Random House in the United States and by Faber and Faber in Britain. Sketching the lineage of Islamic fundamentalism and the histories of rival political ideologies in the Moslem world, Mortimer argued that it was the failure of many nationalist regimes to achieve their political and economic goals during the twentieth century that created the opportunity for a comeback by religious fundamentalists—those who had clung to Islam as a militant ideology in its own right, distinct from secular nationalism.

In two of the case studies in his book, Mortimer considered the central role of Shiism in the Iranian revolution and eval-

*Carnegie trustees and associates at November 1984 meeting in New York*

uated the prospects for an Islamic fundamentalist revival in the Soviet Union. More broadly, he sought to challenge the widespread Western perception of Islam as a hostile and inscrutable monolith.

Together with Carnegie Associates John K. Cooley and Robert Hershman, Mortimer organized a Roundtable on the American Media and the Islamic World, a series of discussions with New York editors and producers. Before resuming his post at the *Times,* he convened a conference of journalists and specialists on the subject of Moslem nationalities in the Soviet Union and wrote on this topic for American newspapers.

William Stivers, a political scientist and the author of *Supremacy and Oil,* an analysis of European diplomacy in the Middle East during the interwar period, conducted research at the Endowment for his book, *Elusive Enemies, Irrelevant Power: America's Confrontation with Revolutionary Change in the Middle East, 1948-83,* scheduled to be published by Macmillan in 1986. For this work, he drew upon previously unexamined documents from U.S. Navy archives. In other writings, Stivers analyzed the failure during the late 1970s of U.S.-Soviet negotiations for a treaty demilitarizing the Indian Ocean. Upon leaving Carnegie, he became director of the

graduate program in West Germany of the University of Southern California's School of International Relations.

Larry L. Fabian, secretary of the Endowment, continued to devote a portion of his time to research and writing on Middle Eastern affairs. His essays on developments in the Middle East have appeared in several journals, including *Foreign Affairs,* which published his overview of events in the region in its 1984 annual world survey.

*Gregory D. Redmon, coordinator of the Carnegie Conference Center*

*In* recent years the Endowment has devoted increasing attention to hemispheric affairs, a commitment whose origins lie in Andrew Carnegie's own deep interest in the strengthening of inter-American relations. Developments in the 1980s have seriously challenged the hemisphere's stability. The amassed foreign debts of several South American countries profoundly strained the international financial system, at times threatening its collapse. Central America appeared suddenly to rival the Middle East as a region of geopolitical consequence. And both of these developments significantly affected

> The single most important cause of instability in Central America is the inability of the economic and military elites to accept responsibility for the collapse of their countries' political and social structures.
>
> Robert E. White,
> *Worldview,*
> December 1981.

*Reception during May 1985 Endowment trustees meeting in Washington at the Pan-American Union, built by Andrew Carnegie and now the headquarters of the Organization of American States*

relations between the United States and its American neighbors.

As tensions began to escalate, Robert S. Leiken, who had spent much of the 1970s teaching and writing in Latin America, came to the Endowment to direct a project on Central America. Early in 1984, a volume of essays edited by Leiken, entitled *Central America: Anatomy of Conflict,* was published by Pergamon Press. Featuring social, political, and diplomatic perspectives on the regional crisis by a range of area specialists, foreign-policy analysts, and former American diplomats, the book was met by favorable reviews in major U.S. and Latin American newspapers and periodicals. It received considerable notice in Congress, in the U.S. policymaking community, and in Latin American capitals at a critical juncture in the Washington policy debate.

Leiken also assembled a group of Washington journalists, editors, and producers for a periodic series of media seminars. During 1984 he organized a two-day conference, cosponsored by the Endowment and the International Institute for Strategic Studies, that addressed West European perspectives on the Central American crisis. The conference papers were edited by Joseph Cirincione and published by Holmes and Meier under the title *Central America and the Western Alliance.*

Leiken wrote widely discussed essays on the crisis in Nicaragua for the *New Republic* and the *New York Review of Books,* and contributed commentaries on U.S. policy in Central America to several newspapers. While engaged in these Carnegie projects, he coedited a collection of primary and secondary source materials, due to be published as a Central America "reader" by Summit Books late in 1985.

Robert E. White arrived at Carnegie after leaving his post as U.S. ambassador to El Salvador. White's extensive diplomatic experience in Latin America and his standing as a critic of U.S. policy there attracted

Robert S. Leiken

Those Sandinistas who have refused to be corrupted recognize that their dreams have turned into a nightmare. One government official told me, "We have given birth to a freak. But we must keep him alive." Yet what is to be done when the freak becomes a menace to its people and neighbors?

Robert S. Leiken,
*The New Republic,*
October 8, 1984.

special attention to his views. His commentaries on aspects of U.S. policy in Central America appeared in many newspapers, including the *Washington Post,* the *New York Times,* the *Los Angeles Times,* and *Newsday.* Journalists regularly consulted White for his views on new developments in the region, and his speeches before professional, academic, and civic groups were widely reported. In congressional testimony, White linked the March 1980 killing of Archbishop Oscar Romero in El Salvador to leading right-wing Salvadoran politicians. Following his tenure at the Endowment, White went on to become Warburg Professor of International Relations at Simmons College and chairman of the Commission on U.S.-Central American Relations at the Center for Development Policy.

Terri Shaw, then the assistant foreign editor of the *Washington Post,* lived in Nicaragua during the period when the Sandinista revolution was being consolidated, yet before the development of tensions with the United States. Upon returning to the United States, she came to the Endowment and wrote about the nature of the Sandinista front and the character of the new society it was attempting to construct.

Peter D. Bell, former president of the Inter-American Foundation and a veteran of many years of professional experience in Latin American development, addressed an array of major issues in hemispheric relations. His frequent writings and speeches encompassed the political consequences of the regional debt crisis and strategies for long-term economic growth; the Contadora multilateral peace initiative in Central America, launched by Mexico, Colombia, Venezuela, and Panama in 1983; the transition from authoritarian to democratic government, especially in Brazil and Uruguay; and the potential for a revival of the once-active "inter-American system."

*Peter D. Bell delivering the keynote address at a Brookings Institution National Issues Forum; at left is Walter E. Beach, of the institution's Advanced Study Program, and at right is Bruce K. MacLaury, president of Brookings*

**L**atin Americans are very much aware of the preponderant weight of the United States in this hemisphere—our economic strength, our military might, and the sheer size of our country. They know that a one percent increase in interest rates here can cost them more than $1 billion in debt service payments.

Peter D. Bell, *Commonweal,* March 22, 1985.

Much of Bell's work on inter-American relations was relevant to his vice-chairmanship of the Inter-American Dialogue, a study group of leading citizens from throughout the Americas convened initially under the auspices of the Woodrow Wilson International Center for Scholars and later of the Aspen Institute for Humanistic Studies. Since 1983 the dialogue has published reports on major inter-American issues after each of its plenary sessions, held every eighteen months. During 1985, in conjunction with Carnegie Associates Robert Leiken and Viron P. Vaky, Bell organized a series of intensive roundtable discussions on current topics in U.S.-Latin American relations. Participants in this monthly forum were drawn mainly from the Washington media, but also included congressional staff aides, area specialists, and occasional Latin American visitors.

Prior to joining the Endowment in 1985, Viron P. Vaky had a notable diplomatic career in Latin America, including service as U.S. ambassador to Costa Rica, Colombia, and Venezuela between 1972 and 1978, and as assistant secretary of state for inter-American affairs during 1978-1979. In his writing and public speaking, Vaky looked into the prospects for the development of a more effective means of regional governance in the Western hemisphere during the coming decade. In the course of this work, Vaky considered many of the key inter-American issues of the day.

Wayne S. Smith, a career diplomat who had just completed a term as chief of mission at the U.S. Interests Section in Havana, examined U.S.-Cuban relations. Drawing on extensive contacts within the Cuban leadership, he attempted to evaluate the possibilities for constructive dialogue between the two countries. In diverse essays, Smith made the case for a new American policy of long-term, gradual engagement with Cuba. Remaining cur-

**S**hould the United States physically intervene in Central America, short of any provocation other than Soviet missile bases, have no doubt that the Latin American reaction will be sharp, adverse, and explosive.

Viron P. Vaky,
remarks to Carnegie
Endowment trustees,
May 1985.

Viron P. Vaky

**P**uerto Rico can regain its competitiveness only if the tax advantages of its existing Commonwealth status are strengthened, not weakened.

Alex W. Maldonado,
report to Carnegie
Endowment trustees, 1983.

rent on Cuban affairs by traveling twice to Havana and renewing his contacts with many officials, including Fidel Castro, Smith concluded in the *New York Times Magazine* that "the Castro of 1984, unlike the Castro of 1960, is a man with whom [the United States] might deal." Smith also prepared essays on the nonaligned movement and on the history of U.S.-Cuban relations, and he wrote articles and commentaries advocating a negotiated solution to the crisis in Central America. He subsequently became professorial lecturer in Latin American studies at the Johns Hopkins University School of Advanced International Studies in Washington.

Taking leave of his post as publisher and executive editor of the Spanish-language daily *El Reportero,* Alex W. Maldonado, one of Puerto Rico's most respected journalists, spent a year at the Endowment studying the unique U.S.-Puerto Rican relationship. He argued for a cessation of the divisive constitutional status debate on the island, contending that the implications of possible Puerto Rican statehood for the rest of the United States are little understood by those who declare the issue simply a matter of self-determination. In light of its comparative poverty and its traditionally strong Democratic party leanings, concluded Maldonado in a *Christian*

*Science Monitor* commentary, a Puerto Rican petition for statehood would force Congress to confront an unprecedented series of complicated economic, political, and cultural issues.

While a Council on Foreign Relations fellow, Richard E. Feinberg, chief Latin American specialist with the State Department's Policy Planning Staff from 1977 to 1979, spent part of a year at the Endowment writing and speaking on U.S. Third World policy, Latin America, and international economic affairs. Since leaving the Endowment, Feinberg has become vice president of the Overseas Development Council.

Wayne S. Smith debates Representative Henry J. Hyde, Republican of Illinois, at the Heritage Foundation; the moderator, center, is Bruce Weinrod

Castro is now a leader who has dealt with the world as it is—and with the Russians as they are—for a quarter of a century. Not surprisingly, then, he gives evidence of a patience and a disposition toward accommodation that were uncharacteristic of him during his early years in power.

Wayne S. Smith,
*Miami News,*
August 9, 1984.

Jorge G. Castañeda, graduate professor of political science at the National Autonomous University of Mexico and a chief adviser to the Mexican government on Central American and Caribbean affairs from 1979 to 1982, came to the Endowment in 1985 to write about Mexican foreign policy, particularly as it relates to developments in Central America.

Exiled Chilean attorney and human rights activist José Zalaquett joined Carnegie in 1985 to examine human rights and the transition from authoritarian rule to democracy in various countries. Before coming to the Endowment, Zalaquett, an internationally recognized legal advocate and scholar, served as deputy secretary general of Amnesty International in London.

Amid indications that ties between Canada and the United States were entering a challenging new period, Anthony Westell, professor of journalism at Carleton University in Ottawa and a columnist for the *Toronto Star,* looked into the shifting economic relationship between the two countries.

In one stage of his research, Westell surveyed sixty Canadian investors in order to outline the factors motivating the expansion of Canadian capital in the United States. He presented his findings in the Ottawa journal *International Perspectives* and before a conference at Carleton University. Westell also examined the U.S.-Canadian energy relationship. Using the Alaska Highway gas pipeline project as a case study, he examined the manner in which the two countries coordinate—or fail to coordinate—economic policy. Before returning to teaching and writing at Carleton, Westell organized an Endowment conference on current research into U.S.-Canadian and U.S.-Canadian-Mexican relations. Late in 1984, a special issue of *International Perspectives* was devoted to a lengthy essay by Westell on Canadian economic integration with the United

José Zalaquett

Through much of Canadian history, it has been easier to blame the United States for problems than to solve them, and this has contributed to the Canadian sense of inferiority.

Anthony Westell,
*International Perspectives,*
November/December 1984.

States, based largely upon research he completed while at Carnegie.

Lise Bissonnette, then assistant editor in chief of the French-language Montreal daily *Le Devoir,* came to the Endowment to write about the special case of U.S. relations with the province of Quebec. Although wary of American ties, the Quebecois have pursued direct dealings with the United States to counterbalance the influence of English-speaking Canada. Bissonnette first addressed the question of whether a form of "double diplomacy" had developed, involving Ottawa, Quebec City, and Washington in a triangular relationship. She published her findings in the *American Review of Canadian Studies* and spoke on them before university conferences in the United States. Bissonnette also undertook a case study of Quebec's electricity exports to the United States. She later convened a conference of Canadian and American economists, public officials, and other specialists to discuss economic issues in U.S.-Quebec relations.

Bissonnette subsequently hosted a documentary on Canadian-American relations on the French-language national television network, Radio Canada. The ninety-minute program emphasized American reactions to Canadian nationalism and its effects on proposals for further cooperation between the two countries. Bissonnette later became editor of *Le Devoir.*

*Jenny C. Grimsley, library assistant, and David Weiner, staff assistant on Carnegie Anniversary Project*

> **W**hile the level of Quebec's foreign dealings is undoubtedly higher than that of any other Canadian province, it is far from certain, except in the very particular case of France, that Quebec has departed from the style and substance of foreign activity pursued by the other "non-independentist" provinces of Canada.
>
> Lise Bissonnette,
> *American Review of Canadian Studies,*
> Spring 1981

*C*arnegie associates have in recent years undertaken projects inquiring into the politics or international relations of several crucial subregions of Asia.

When the Soviet Union invaded Afghanistan at the end of 1979, few Americans were more qualified to comment on the event than Selig S. Harrison. For some time he had been examining the phenomenon of Baluch nationalism and, in particular, the separatist threat posed by the Baluch minority in Pakistan. The installation of a Soviet-backed regime in Afghanistan in 1979 suddenly placed this matter at the center of a profound regional crisis.

*Selig S. Harrison*

**S**hould the United States enlarge its military support of Pakistan, Indian hostility to the American presence in the Indian Ocean would be likely to increase, together with Indian reliance on Soviet support for Indian naval development.

Selig S. Harrison,
congressional testimony,
February 27, 1985.

Harrison's volume *In Afghanistan's Shadow: Baluch Nationalism and Soviet Temptations* assessed the potential of the movement for an independent greater Baluchistan embracing strategically located areas in Pakistan and Iran, around the Arabian Sea.

In the months following the Soviet invasion, Harrison responded to many requests—from Europe as well as the United States—for articles, speeches, media briefings, radio and television commentary, congressional testimony, and consultations with government officials. In an article in *Foreign Policy,* he offered an account of the Soviet Union's motivations and explored the prospects for a negotiated settlement based upon a neutralized Afghanistan.

Recognizing the regional implications of the Afghan crisis, Harrison increasingly turned his attention to the question of American policy toward Pakistan and India. Testifying before the House Foreign Affairs Committee, he cautioned that the Reagan administration's proposed bolstering of Pakistan's armed forces could have an adverse effect on U.S.-Indian relations and ultimately could even lead to a new Indo-Pakistani war.

In 1982 Harrison organized a conference on U.S.-Indian relations, which set in motion plans for an Indo-American Task Force on the Indian Ocean. Jointly sponsored by the Endowment and the Indian Institute of Defense Studies and Analyses, with support from the Ford Foundation, the task force consisted of six Americans and six Indians—political analysts, military specialists, and former officials. They met in New Delhi over a five-day period in 1984 to discuss the escalating arms race in the Indian Ocean and Persian Gulf and the reduction of the Indo-U.S. tensions that had resulted from the American military presence in the region. The task force report was published together with key excerpts from the group's discussions in

*Trustees' working session at the Carnegie Conference Center in Washington*

the summer of 1985. A collection of the working papers, edited by Harrison, was scheduled to appear in hardcover early in 1986.

In congressional testimony, seminars, and conferences, and in later writings, Harrison returned to the Afghanistan question, focusing on the course of the faltering United Nations negotiating initiative. In March 1984, during a trip through South Asia, he met with Babrak Karmal, the Soviet-backed Afghan leader.

Harrison has also continued to monitor developments relating to China's offshore oil activity, following up on the research that led to the publication in 1977 of his Carnegie study *China, Oil, and Asia: Conflict Ahead?* He delivered the keynote address at the Offshore China '81 conference, a gathering of some 2,500 foreign oil-industry executives, Chinese officials, and specialists in Guangzhou.

Christopher Van Hollen's tenure at the Endowment coincided with one of the most eventful periods in South and Southwest Asia and the Persian Gulf during the postwar era. As a regular commentator for television news broadcasts and a frequent participant in academic conferences and colloquiums, Van Hollen, former U.S. ambassador to Sri Lanka and, prior to that, deputy assistant secretary of state for Near

*Trustees Marion R. Fremont-Smith and Edson W. Spencer*

Eastern and South Asian affairs, considered American foreign-policy challenges in each of these uneasy regions.

His case study of the evolution and regional repercussions of the U.S. "tilt" toward Pakistan during the 1971 Indo-Pakistani war appeared in the journal *Asian Survey*. His analysis of the ineffectiveness of U.S. legislative sanctions in the effort to control South Asian nuclear programs was published in the *Washington Quarterly*. In *Foreign Affairs* and other publications, Van Hollen challenged the Reagan administration's promotion of a "strategic consensus" in the Gulf region and Southwest Asia. After leaving the En-

dowment, he was appointed director of the American Institute for Islamic Affairs.

S. Nihal Singh, editor in chief of the *Indian Express,* considered several aspects of India's most important international relationship—that with the Soviet Union. In order to place this relationship in an illuminating context, he first surveyed the recent history of India's strained relations with the United States and examined the origins of the 1971 Indo-Soviet "friendship treaty." Singh then looked at trade between India and the Soviet Union, increasingly the most crucial and contentious element in Indo-Soviet relations. He concluded his project with a look at the

*Christopher Van Hollen*

The Americans and the Soviets each have proxies to speak for them at nonaligned gatherings. In this battle for the hearts and minds of the nonaligned, the West now has the advantage.

S. Nihal Singh,
*Newsweek International,*
March 26, 1984.

political role of the pro-Moscow Communist party of India. Upon completing his term with Carnegie, Singh moved to Paris to undertake a book project sponsored by the Twentieth Century Fund.

After retiring as vice president of the Asia Society and director of its Washington Center, Robert W. Barnett worked on a range of Asian security issues at the Endowment. In 1984 Pergamon-Brassey's published his study of Japanese defense strategy, *Beyond War: Japan's Concept of Comprehensive National Security.* Barnett organized his book around conversations with current and former policymakers, military officials, and scholars in Japan, other Asian countries, and the United States. For the Japanese, he found, "comprehensive security" signifies an ambitious, nuanced strategy for forestalling, preventing, or limiting war—a strategy that emphasizes carefully calibrated economic and political diplomacy, rather than the build-up of armaments.

Barnett concluded that both regional security and Japanese pacifist principles would be best served if Japan were to promote itself in the area of its greatest comparative advantage, "knowledge." Thus he recommended that Japan build "coordinated defense services" for an "elaborately comprehensive high-technology" intelligence capability—that it become the eyes and ears of the alliance.

Yoshihisa Komori, a Japanese journalist and author whose reporting of defense issues at home earned his newspaper, *Mainichi,* the Japanese equivalent of the Pulitzer Prize, concentrated on the emergence of a national security debate in Japan in the early 1980s. In order to comprehend how pressures for a Japanese defense build-up would affect Japan's security ties with the Western alliance, Komori carried out an extensive series of interviews with policymakers and opinion leaders in both Japan and the United States. In the *New York Times,* he

*Robert W. Barnett*

The Japanese public's attitude toward nuclear weapons is changing significantly. The findings of recent opinion polls probably startled outsiders accustomed to hearing of the "nuclear allergy"—the national aversion to nuclear arms—which Japan's news media have depicted as very nearly a permanent fixture.

Yoshihisa Komori,
*New York Times,*
November 5, 1981.

described Japanese popular attitudes toward nuclear weapons. For the prestigious Japanese journals *Chuo Koron* and *Gendai,* he wrote about recent American perspectives on Japan's defense effort and on the origins of its constitutional prohibition of "war potential." These essays were subsequently included in two volumes of his writings published in Japan, where Komori resumed writing for *Mainichi.*

As Carnegie Associate Marvin C. Ott observed, with the election of Yasuhiro Nakasone in 1982, Japan acquired a prime minister who was determined that his country establish for itself an international role commensurate with its economic power. Ott, former director of congressional and institutional relations at the U.S. Office of Technology Assessment, studied the unprecedented foreign-policy activism of the Nakasone years.

His primary focus was Japanese policy in the Middle East, where energy and economic interests had dictated a more aggressive role. In journal articles and op-ed pieces, Ott surveyed the origins and current orientation of Japan's Middle East posture and their implications for U.S. policy in the region. He also wrote about Japanese-American technological collaboration and the diplomatic situation in Indochina. Following his Carnegie project, Ott joined the senior staff of the U.S. Senate Select Committee on Intelligence, assuming responsibility for Asia and the Pacific.

Evelyn Colbert, deputy assistant secretary of state for East Asian and Pacific affairs from 1978 to 1980, spent time at the Endowment pursuing her lifelong interest in East and Southeast Asian history and current affairs. A thirty-year State Department veteran and the author of the volume *Southeast Asia in International Politics, 1941-56,* Colbert concentrated on regional security in Indochina. Her monograph *Power Balance and Security in Indochina* was published by the Secu-

**K**ey Western European policymakers are disturbed by the prospect of a U.S.-Japanese science and technology juggernaut that would make Europe a technological backwater.

Marvin C. Ott, *Los Angeles Times,* January 2, 1985.

*Evelyn Colbert*

*Marvin C. Ott*

rity Conference on Asia and the Pacific. After leaving Carnegie, she became professorial lecturer in Asian studies at the Johns Hopkins University School of Advanced International Studies in Washington.

The 1983 assassination of opposition leader Benigno Aquino upon his return from exile propelled the Philippines into the international headlines, where it stayed for much of the 1983-1985 period. In the aftermath of Aquino's death, American policy toward the authoritarian Marcos regime came under intense scrutiny. In 1985 the Endowment invited Richard J. Kessler, formerly of Georgetown University's Center for Strategic and International Studies, to examine the conflicting claims of American security and democratic change in the Philippines. In a series of journal and newspaper commentaries, and in a 1985 monograph, Kessler evaluated the character and potential reform of the Philippine military, the prospects of the New People's Army communist insurgency, and the role of the Philippines in safeguarding American economic and security interests in Southeast Asia. He also addressed the impact of Philippine development policies on domestic stability and the value of foreign economic assistance in effecting political change in the Philippines.

**P**olarization in Washington of the policy debate on the Philippines can only benefit the Marcos regime. Far better to begin crafting a bipartisan agreement on policy, presenting a united front to President Marcos, a man long practiced at exploiting American schisms.

Richard J. Kessler,
Baltimore *Sun,*
April 10, 1985.

*Richard J. Kessler*

*I*n its Africa projects during the first half of the 1980s, the Endowment sought to address issues that, from both humanitarian and political perspectives, have dominated the affairs of that troubled continent.

John de St. Jorre, a journalist and author of several books on African affairs, including the 1977 Carnegie volume *A House Divided: South Africa's Uncertain Future,* returned to the Endowment to write on the diplomatic situation in southern Africa. In specialized publications such as *Africa Report,* and in general periodicals and newspapers, de St. Jorre focused on the international, regional, and internal issues underlying the tensions between South Africa and its neighbors. He also probed the Reagan administration's "constructive engagement" policy, South Africa's regional destabilization efforts, and its 1984 accords with Angola and Mozambique, as well as the multilateral shuttle negotiations over a formula for securing the independence of Namibia. De St. Jorre resumed free-lance writing in New York after leaving Carnegie.

Jack Shepherd, a journalist and award-winning author who had also completed a book, *The Politics of Starvation,* while an associate at the Endowment during the

John de St. Jorre

**P**eople who are forced to go down on their knees to sue for peace tend neither to forget nor to forgive the humiliation. Pax Pretoriana may look logical on the surface, but it is riddled with internal contradictions. Although it may produce a temporary rapprochement in the region, it is unlikely to usher in an era of permanent peace.

John de St. Jorre,
*The New Republic,*
April 2, 1984.

1970s, returned in 1984 to examine food aid and agriculture in sub-Saharan Africa. Since the start of his project coincided with the onset of Africa's second massive famine in a ten-year period, Shepherd initially monitored the short-term food emergency—analyzing its causes and commenting on relief efforts in numerous articles and frequent interviews. In later writings, Shepherd studied Reagan administration policies on long-term development assistance to Africa. The impact of foreign assistance on African economic development was the subject of his major essay for the April 1985 issue of the *Atlantic*. Shepherd returned to book projects upon leaving the Endowment in 1985.

John K. Cooley, a veteran of twenty-five years of reporting in the Middle East and North Africa, spent a year at the Endowment writing on North African issues. In articles and commentaries for the *Washington Post*, the *Christian Science Monitor*, and the *Los Angeles Times*, among others, he inquired into the course of the war in the Western Sahara, the Palestinian conflict, the politics of succession in Morocco and Tunisia, and the regional influence of Libyan leader Muammar el-Qaddafi's Soviet-backed, radical Moslem regime. Qaddafi was also the focus of Cooley's *Foreign Policy* article "The Libyan Menace." The *Middle East Journal* carried his analysis of news reporting from the Middle East.

Cooley's book on Qaddafi's rise, *Libyan Sandstorm*, written before he came to the Endowment, was published by Holt, Rinehart and Winston soon after he left. He later became an ABC news correspondent based in London.

Pauline H. Baker, a former staff member of the U.S. Senate Foreign Relations Committee with extensive university teaching experience in Nigeria, was selected to work at the Endowment in 1986 on American policy toward Africa. She also planned to examine Africa's econom-

The large-scale outpouring of emergency food to Africa is a worthwhile and dramatic first step toward saving lives. The crucial next step, which must be taken now, is to determine what long-term development aid will best lay the groundwork for the recovery of Africa's environment, agriculture, and people.

Jack Shepherd,
*New York Times*,
January 10, 1985.

*Jack Shepherd, foreground, with Thomas L. Hughes*

ic crisis and the prospects for fundamental change in South Africa.

After leaving National Public Radio, where he had hosted "All Things Considered" and other public affairs programs, Sanford J. Ungar came to the Endowment to direct the Carnegie Anniversary Project, established for the purpose of commemorating the seventy-fifth anniversary of the Endowment's founding in 1910. The centerpiece of this project was a volume of essays on postwar American foreign policy entitled *Estrangement: America and the World,* published by Oxford University Press in 1985.

**M**uammar el-Qaddafi is being inflated beyond his true power or stature. What is pumping him up is chiefly the almost hysterical, yet seemingly ineffectual, American abuse heaped upon him since *Newsweek* magazine dubbed him "the most dangerous man in the world."

John K. Cooley,
*Los Angeles Times,*
November 1, 1981.

*Pauline H. Baker*

39

Each of the book's dozen authors explored a set of events or themes that, in retrospect, could be seen to have contributed significantly to current American difficulties in the world. By reaching backward and forward across the postwar period—drawing connections among distinct events and policies where they had not always been recognized before—the authors tried to cast familiar episodes in American foreign policy in a new and revealing light. In addition to Ungar, who wrote the introduction, the book's contributors included Robert Dallek, Robert J. Donovan, Donald F. McHenry, J. Bryan Hehir, Godfrey Hodgson, Lester C.

Thurow, Ali A. Mazrui, Philip L. Geyelin, James Chace, Frances FitzGerald, and Richard H. Ullman.

Ungar, former managing editor of *Foreign Policy,* also worked on African issues. While completing the research and writing for his 1985 Simon and Schuster book

*Africa: The People and Politics of an Emerging Continent,* which he had begun several years earlier, Ungar frequently contributed commentaries on major African developments and U.S. policy in Africa to newspapers and magazines throughout the United States.

*Sanford J. Ungar with the Rev. J. Bryan Hehir, one of the contributors to the volume of essays published on the occasion of the Endowment's seventy-fifth anniversary,* Estrangement: America and the World

The Endowment has attempted to enhance the understanding of some of the consequences of growing international interdependence, often through study groups or roundtable programs that draw upon the contributions of individuals with diverse backgrounds and expertise.

Developments in the international economy during the past decade have placed severe strains on the institutional arrangements established after World War II. Accordingly, observed Carnegie Associate Catherine Gwin, the institutional management of international economic affairs in key areas, such as currency, fin-

If developing countries are going to achieve satisfactory rates of growth over the course of the next decade, they will have to find new sources of finance in addition to loans from commercial banks, and they will have to become less dependent on external financing.

Catherine Gwin,
*Beyond Debt Crisis Management:
An International Institutional Response,*
1984.

*Catherine Gwin*

ance, and trade, must be made more responsive to new global economic trends. Finishing a term as North-South issues coordinator with the U.S. International Development Cooperation Agency, she looked at impediments to the successful conduct of international economic diplomacy and investigated ways of improving multilateral economic management.

Gwin organized and led a Carnegie Endowment Study Group on International Financial Cooperation, a working seminar of business people, scholars, and public officials who met monthly for nearly a year. The group's primary objective was to explore how the policies and practices of

*Ronald Steel*

the World Bank and the International Monetary Fund might evolve in ways that would promote over the long term a more stable international financial system. In preparing the final report, *Beyond Debt Crisis Management: An International Institutional Response,* Gwin drew upon the analyses and recommendations that emerged from the group's deliberations. At the conclusion of her project she became an independent consultant for several institutions in New York, including the Ford and Rockefeller foundations, the Asia Society, and Columbia University.

Ronald Steel, the author of acclaimed books on American foreign policy and of

Europeans want equality while we expect obedience. But the more we force them to pay their own way, the more disobedient they will be. There is no way out of this dilemma that is compatible with NATO as we know it.

Ronald Steel,
*Vanity Fair,*
March 1983.

the award-winning biography *Walter Lippmann and the American Century,* undertook a review of U.S. commitments and alliances around the world. Steel considered whether the global network of alliances and security relationships the United States had entered into after World War II, when it held unprecedented wealth and military power, was still necessary—or sustainable—at a time when its economic position had declined, its allies were more prosperous, and its ability to determine events was sharply limited.

Among his articles on this topic were an essay for *Vanity Fair* on America's assertiveness in the 1980s and one for *Harper's*

on the U.S. troop commitment to NATO. After leaving the Endowment, Steel continued to pursue these themes at the Woodrow Wilson International Center for Scholars in Washington, subsequently returning to free-lance writing and lecturing.

As both voluntary and forced population flows have grown in recent years, immigration and refugee matters—long considered the exclusive province of domestic policymakers—have increasingly been taken up in foreign-policy debates. Michael S. Teitelbaum, a demographer with professional experience in economic development and in Congress, analyzed the interaction of international population

movements and the formulation of foreign policy. In addition to writing for journals and newspapers, he spoke on these issues before numerous professional, academic, and public audiences. He was frequently consulted by congressional staff members and State Department officials concerning immigration and refugee matters, and he coordinated a conference in Italy for European foreign-policy and immigration specialists. Finishing his Endowment project, Teitelbaum joined the staff of the Alfred P. Sloan Foundation in New York.

C. Fred Bergsten, assistant secretary of the treasury for international affairs from

*Michael S. Teitelbaum*

*C. Fred Bergsten addresses the Mid-Atlantic Club at the Carnegie Conference Center*

1977 to 1981, and the author or editor of more than ten books, addressed three major international economic topics during a year at Carnegie: the evolution and management of the emerging multiple reserve currency system; U.S. policy toward the multilateral development banks; and the competitive position of the United States in world markets. An internationally respected political economist, Bergsten was frequently asked to comment on economic issues for American and foreign media. While at Carnegie, he laid the groundwork for launching a new organization, the Institute for International Economics, initially backed by the German Marshall Fund of the United States. He became the institute's first director in 1982.

Charles Maechling, Jr., an international legal scholar, wrote extensively on law-related issues while with the Endowment. Latin America was the region to which he paid the most attention, emphasizing human rights questions in particular. Maechling's influential critique of Reagan administration human rights policy was published in *Foreign Policy,* and his articles on human rights, terrorism and political violence, U.S. policy in Central America, the international debt crisis, and the law of the sea appeared in the *New York Times,* the *Christian Science Monitor,*

*Trustees Charles W. Bailey II, below, and Governor Rafael Hernández-Colón of Puerto Rico, right*

the *Los Angeles Times,* the *Foreign Service Journal,* and the U.S. Army War College journal *Parameters.* Maechling also participated in panels, conferences, and media interviews concerning human rights, sea law, and other international legal topics. He served on the board of directors of Citizens for Ocean Law. After leaving the Endowment, he became a visiting teaching fellow at Cambridge University.

As coordinator during 1976-1977 of the Group of 77 bloc of developing countries at the United Nations, Pakistani diplomat Mian Qadrud-Din played a role in the international economic negotiations that took place under U.N. auspices between

**I**f extended to every variation of insurgency, armed rebellion and civil warfare, terrorism as a concept loses meaning and becomes a propaganda tool to stigmatize an enemy.

Charles Maechling, Jr.,
*New York Times,*
June 27, 1984

*Charles Maechling, Jr.*

the countries of the "North" and the "South." After joining the Endowment, Qadrud-Din, who had also been the Middle East director-general of the Pakistan Ministry of Foreign Affairs, organized a Carnegie Forum on Development Issues, in the hope of contributing to the resumption of a useful North-South dialogue. These sessions brought together senior U.N. diplomats to discuss development issues with special guests drawn from international finance and development institutions, various governments' foreign- and economic-policy departments, the private sector, and the academic world. Qadrud-Din later became special assistant to the undersecretary general of the United Nations.

Upon leaving the U.S. Treasury Department, after working on trade and international energy policy for several administrations, Jeffrey J. Schott launched another of the Endowment's projects in international political economy: trade in services—shipping and civil aviation, telecommunications, travel and tourism, and financial, consulting, and engineering services. Schott investigated the likely policy initiatives and institutional reforms required for the establishment of a set of international rules in this area, as well as the prospects for multilateral negotiations on such a regime.

*J. Daniel O'Flaherty*

*Jeffrey J. Schott*

As part of this effort, he led a Carnegie Roundtable on Trade in Services, an informal discussion forum with roughly twenty-five participants. Schott also published articles on trade issues and, along with Gary C. Hufbauer, wrote a detailed assessment of the utility of international economic leverage, *Economic Sanctions Reconsidered: History and Current Policy.* This volume was published by the Institute for International Economics, where Schott became a research associate after leaving Carnegie.

The relationship between international finance and foreign policy was the subject of a Carnegie Roundtable on Banking and Foreign Policy, organized by J. Daniel O'Flaherty. The purpose of this two-year series of meetings was to provide a forum for members of the New York financial community to meet with prominent foreign-policy specialists for discussion of political and economic issues. Participants included New York bankers, stock analysts, consultants, corporate lawyers, and financial journalists.

Subsequently, O'Flaherty established a Carnegie Lawyers Roundtable on Foreign Policy, a similar forum whose participants were drawn from the younger ranks of the New York legal community. Its objective was to introduce promising young attorneys to substantive international policy questions.

O'Flaherty also coordinated the Endowment's highly regarded intern program. Each year, ten to twelve interns are selected from a group of more than a hundred nominees from colleges and universities throughout the United States. Every intern is assigned for a six-month term to a Carnegie program, where he or she is given responsibilities for research, editing, and writing. *Foreign Policy* magazine and the Arms Control Association regularly employ several editorial and research interns every year; other interns provide valuable assistance to special projects, panels, and

Karin M. Lissakers

Substituting more costly loans for old loans (rescheduling), then adding another $4 to $5 billion in still costlier new credits, seems a curious way to help countries which have too much debt to begin with. From the bankers' point of view it can only make sense if they assume that the risk is not theirs but someone else's.

Karin M. Lissakers,
Baltimore *Sun,*
May 23, 1983.

roundtables. Many of the men and women who have held these positions have gone on to play significant roles in American public affairs and journalism.

Upon leaving Carnegie in 1984, O'Flaherty joined the Group of Thirty, a private international forum established to study global economic problems.

Karin M. Lissakers, an economist with experience in Congress and the State Department, concentrated on the foreign-policy implications of private commercial banking during her tenure with the Endowment. In particular, she sought to draw conclusions about the impact on American foreign policy of the overseas activities of U.S. banks, especially in their lending to foreign governments. In an article for *Foreign Policy* that received wide coverage in the American press, Lissakers analyzed the freezing of Iranian financial assets in the United States during the 1979-1981 hostage crisis.

The political consequences of the extension of credit to Poland and other Soviet-bloc countries by private Western banks were the subject of articles and press interviews by Lissakers during the Polish debt crisis. In subsequent writings on the 1982-1983 Mexican debt emergency, Lissakers examined the vulnerability of the world banking system to disruption resulting from the large international losses of a few major lenders. After completing her project, Lissakers began work on a book on international banking and subsequently became an adjunct professor at the Columbia University School of International and Public Affairs.

David Lascelles, formerly the New York bureau chief of the *Financial Times* of London, focused on the question of bank-government relations. He participated in several seminars, discussion groups, and public affairs broadcasts concerning the politicization of international lending. For the *Banker* magazine he wrote an article on the U.S. government's handling of the

## Colleges and Universities Attended by Recent Carnegie Endowment Interns

Amherst College
Boston University
Brandeis University
Brown University
Carleton College
Clark University
Columbia University
Cornell University
Dartmouth College
Duke University
Georgetown University
Hampshire College
Harvard University
Harvey Mudd College
Haverford College
Johns Hopkins University
Lawrence University
Louisiana State University
McGill University
Miami University
Michigan State University
Mount Holyoke College
Northwestern University
Oberlin College
Ohio Wesleyan University
Pomona College
Princeton University
Reed College
Sarah Lawrence College
Southwestern University
Stanford University
State University of New York, Albany
Swarthmore College
Texas Christian University
Tufts University
University of California, Berkeley
University of California, Santa Cruz
University of Georgia
University of Maryland
University of Michigan
University of Minnesota
University of North Carolina
University of Notre Dame
University of the Pacific
University of Virginia
University of Wisconsin, LaCrosse
University of Wisconsin, Madison
Vanderbilt University
Wesleyan University
Williams College
Xavier University
Yale University

*Richard Gilmore*

role of private banks in the Third World debt crisis. In other articles, he compared the lending records of U.S. and foreign banks and advocated the creation by lender countries of a coherent and balanced international banking policy. Lascelles subsequently returned to the London headquarters of the *Financial Times,* where he covered banking issues.

Continuing a project he started with a Rockefeller Foundation grant, international political economist Richard Gilmore looked into the structural, economic, and political character of the international grain trading system. In view of the efficiency costs and welfare risks associated with the existing international grain trade, Gilmore attempted to develop policy recommendations for a new grain regime that would help stabilize prices, increase agricultural production, guarantee importers' food security, and harmonize the major national marketing systems. He set out these proposals in his book *A Poor Harvest: The Clash of Policies and Interests in the Grain Trade,* published by Longman and later translated into Japanese. Gilmore founded a consulting firm after he left Carnegie.

Upon leaving the British Broadcasting Corporation after thirty years, many of them spent as director of BBC operations in the United States, David Webster arrived at Carnegie in 1985 to explore international communications issues. Webster concerned himself particularly with the rapidly expanding satellite-based technologies that are leading to a restructuring of the communications industry, fragmenting audiences, and spurring the growth of transnational telecommunications systems, all with significant international consequences. In his own research, and in collaboration with other specialists, he evaluated the international political, cultural, and financial impact of these applications on the cutting edge of satellite communications technology.

Airpower and missiles completely changed military doctrine just as satellite technology destroys the traditional geography of mass media.

David Webster,
remarks to Carnegie
Endowment trustees,
May 1985.

*David Webster*

The Endowment has sponsored several projects that looked into crucial aspects of the relationship between domestic politics and American foreign policy. These projects have focused on some of the deeper currents in the domestic political culture, seeking to render more comprehensible America's unique interaction of the media, Congress, and public opinion with the traditional foreign-policymaking machinery.

I. M. Destler, a political scientist with substantial experience in the public sector, undertook an ambitious five-year project inquiring into the impact on American foreign policy of the relationship between Congress and the executive branch. He monitored executive-congressional interaction over such policy dilemmas as the SALT II debate, trade issues, conflict in Central America, and foreign economic- and military-assistance appropriations. A prolific contributor of articles and essays to scholarly volumes, periodicals, and journals, such as *Political Science Quarterly,* the *Washington Quarterly,* and *Foreign Policy,* Destler's case studies and theoretical writings established him as a public policy specialist with a national reputation.

> **A**mericans want two things that often prove incompatible in practice: *democratic government* (involving ongoing competition among a range of U.S. interests and perspectives) and *effective foreign policy* (which requires settling on specific goals and pursuing them consistently).
>
> I.M. Destler,
> essay in *Congress Reconsidered,*
> 1985.

*I. M. Destler*

In conjunction with Alton Frye, Washington director of the Council on Foreign Relations, Destler coordinated a Joint Discussion Group on Executive-Congressional Relations in Foreign Policy. Cosponsored by the Endowment and the Council, and chaired by Thomas L. Hughes and later by former White House counsel Lloyd N. Cutler, this group of government officials, congressional staff members, and academic specialists met regularly over a five-year period.

Destler also organized a series of seminars, cosponsored by the Brookings Institution, for Japanese correspondents based in Washington. Each session featured an American specialist or policymaker who addressed an issue of special concern to the Japanese. Destler became a senior fellow at the Institute for International Economics after departing from Carnegie.

Frank C. Ballance, author of *The Political and Economic Crisis in Southern Africa,* looked at aspects of congressional involvement in the making of U.S. policy toward the Third World. Having served on congressional staffs and in the executive branch, he focused primarily on the politics of the annual deliberations over the American foreign aid bill, the major vehicle Congress uses to state and control Third World policies. Ballance considered

*Trustees, from left at table, George N. Lindsay, Jean Kennedy Smith, William J. Perry, John B. Slaughter, Robert F. Goheen, Donald B. Straus, and Wesley W. Posvar*

*Frank C. Ballance*

Congress's role in shaping and revitalizing U.S. aid policy in the 1970s and sought to understand congressional perceptions of the Third World. Experiences in the field, particularly in Africa and Asia, led Ballance to write about many of these aid and development issues from the perspective of the recipient countries, focusing especially on the developmental challenges faced by Zimbabwe. Ballance went into independent consulting after leaving Carnegie

While on leave from his position as chairman of the political science department at Colgate University, Robert H. Johnson spent a year at the Endowment considering the relationship between American domestic politics and the policy of détente with the Soviet Union during the 1970s. In an effort to explain the difficulty in sustaining public support for this mixed policy of competition and cooperation with Moscow, Johnson evaluated the domestic psychological and cultural reverberations of developments in the U.S.-Soviet relationship. This fusion of domestic political and cultural analysis with diplomatic studies led to two essays, one on the international varieties of populism for *International Organization,* and the other an analysis in *Foreign Affairs* of the recurring "myth" of national security peril. Johnson resumed teaching at the conclusion of his Endowment project and later returned to Washington as a visiting fellow at the Overseas Development Council.

Harry J. Shaw's project on the role of security assistance in American foreign policy grew directly out of his experience as chief of the international security affairs branch of the U.S. Office of Management and Budget. In that capacity, Shaw was responsible for preparing the foreign military assistance component of the president's annual budget. At the Endowment, he focused on what he considered the most significant characteristic of American security assistance during this

*Harry J. Shaw*

*Robert H. Johnson*

There are striking parallels between the new populism of the developing countries, reflected in their demands for a new international economic order, and the older agrarian populism of nineteenth century America.

Robert H. Johnson,
*International Organization,*
Winter 1983.

decade: the degree to which it has come to be dominated, not by military and economic considerations, but by the "short-term exigencies of diplomacy and political influence buying."

One of Shaw's case studies was the American military and economic assistance relationship with Israel. In addition to writing newspaper commentaries on this topic, he testified about U.S. security assistance policies in the Middle East before the House Foreign Appropriations Subcommittee and addressed a conference of American Jewish scholars sponsored by B'nai B'rith.

Terry L. Deibel, professor of national security policy at the National War College in Washington and a former Carnegie associate, rejoined the Endowment in 1985 to investigate the content and geographic patterns of U.S. security commitments in the Third World.

Kenneth Longmyer came to the Endowment in the spring of 1985, while on leave from the State Department as a Pearson Fellow. He examined the participation of black Americans in the formulation and

execution of U.S. foreign policy, seeking to explain the relationship between their domestic political role and their relative lack of interest in American foreign policy. In diverse essays and addresses Longmyer attempted to evaluate the foreign priorities of black Americans and the results of their infrequent efforts to influence foreign policy.

In his project on the press, government, and foreign policy, John H. Trattner, who had just served as spokesman for the State

*Terry L. Deibel*

*Kenneth Longmyer*

Department, used his extensive experience in official press relations to help clarify the relationship between American journalism and foreign policy. His writings on the influence of foreign affairs reporting, the practice of official press relations, and the policy impact of public diplomacy appeared in several journals and newspapers, including the *Washington Quarterly* and the *New York Times*. Trattner has been a U.S. Senate press aide and a public policy consultant since leaving the Endowment.

Journalist Robert Hershman explored the impact on foreign policy of television news coverage. Focusing on the Iran hostage crisis and the rise of the Solidarity union in Poland, Hershman looked at the increasingly prominent role of academic experts in news reporting, relations between governments and media during protracted crises, and the volatile effects of television's unique personalization of foreign events. He wrote about Iran for the *Columbia Journalism Review,* the *Christian Science Monitor,* and *Television Quarterly.* He later joined ABC News.

*John H. Trattner*

*Mary J. Child, project staff*

$F$ounded in 1971 to enhance public understanding of nuclear weapons and the contribution arms limitation can make to national security, the Arms Control Association (ACA) is a separately incorporated, nonpartisan, tax-exempt organization with a national membership and its own program staff and independent board of directors. But ACA periodically undertakes joint ventures with the Carnegie Endowment.

Under the guidance of William H. Kincade, executive director from 1977 to 1984, and of Spurgeon M. Keeny, Jr., who succeeded Kincade in 1985, ACA's pro-

grams grew in proportion with the unprecedented increase in public and official concern over arms control during the 1980s. The quality of the association's policy analysis, public information services, media outreach, and educational programs has given it a unique role in American public affairs.

ACA has steadily expanded its programs and capabilities to meet the rising public demand for arms limitation information and analysis. Since the late 1970s it has sought to fill this need by sponsoring topical briefings for the Washington media. These regularly scheduled, well-attended sessions provide national security and

*Spurgeon M. Keeny, Jr.*

diplomatic correspondents with authoritative background analysis of current and emerging arms control issues.

During 1983 and 1984, in an effort to reach beyond the traditional public affairs community on the East Coast, ACA initiated a series of day-long press seminars for selected editors and reporters in major regional media centers like Atlanta, Chicago, and San Francisco. The association also produces "editorial advisories"—brief, intensive analyses of current issues that are distributed to editors and producers around the country.

Staff members and interns further meet the demand for factual interpretation and analysis by answering more than a hundred information requests each month from specialists, congressional aides, and concerned citizens, often drawing upon the extensive holdings in the ACA research library. The effort to reach the public frequently takes association board members and senior staff on the road to address diverse audiences on crucial issues on the arms control agenda. ACA representatives are consulted or interviewed by many of the Washington-based national news and public affairs outlets, as well as by local media.

The ACA bulletin, *Arms Control Today,* is a respected monthly forum for the discussion of arms control and security-related topics and research resources. Each issue features at least one major article on noteworthy developments or policy questions written by a prominent scholar, analyst, or policymaker. Early in 1985, Robert Travis Scott took over the editorship of *Arms Control Today* from Jeffrey D. Porro, who had edited it since 1980. *The Race for Security,* a reader assembling some of the most significant articles appearing in *Arms Control Today* during the 1980s, was edited by Scott and set for publication by Lexington Books late in 1985.

ACA personnel have written and edited numerous books, monographs, and jour-

nal and newspaper articles on the full range of arms limitation issues. ACA President Herbert Scoville, Jr.'s book *MX: Prescription for Disaster,* published by the MIT Press, offered one of the definitive critiques of that controversial missile program. Board members Gerard C. Smith and Robert S. McNamara have written ground-breaking articles for *Foreign Affairs* and other journals on the question of "no first-use" of nuclear weapons and the military utility of nuclear forces. ACA staff contribute topical articles and commentaries to major newspapers and periodicals, and the association occasionally supports the publication of research by outside specialists and organizations.

ACA often produces detailed studies of arms limitation issues that are the focus of special public and official attention. For example, in 1984 it assessed two official U.S. reports on Soviet compliance with existing arms control agreements. Staff and board members have also prepared a survey of arms control options for the 1980s, a technical study of MX missile-basing plans, a model proposal for the START and INF negotiations, a historical analysis of the postwar superpower competition, and evaluations of the U.S.-Soviet military balance.

In another major undertaking, the association played a key role in organizing several national organizations and nearly fifty prominent individual sponsors into a National Campaign to Save the ABM Treaty, a public education coalition. The campaign's efforts were boosted early in 1985 when ACA General Counsel John B. Rhinelander, Associate Director for Research and Analysis Thomas K. Longstreth, and John E. Pike of the Federation of American Scientists collaborated on a report, "The Impact of U.S. and Soviet Ballistic Missile Defense Programs on the ABM Treaty." When the planned modernization of U.S. nuclear forces in 1985 threatened

*Arms Control Association staff meeting, including former Deputy Director Julia A. Moore, at end of table, and Jeffrey D. Porro, former editor of* Arms Control Today, *foreground*

*Arms Control Association senior staff, from left, Associate Director Robert Travis Scott, Executive Director Spurgeon M. Keeny, Jr., Deputy Director Jack W. Mendelsohn, and Associate Director Thomas K. Longstreth*

to contravene key components of the un-ratified 1979 SALT II agreement, ACA published a comprehensive evaluation of the treaty that presented a strong case for continued voluntary U.S. and Soviet adherence to its provisions.

Several important volumes have resulted from arms control conferences sponsored or organized by ACA. Two such volumes emerged from the annual "New Faces" conferences for security specialists under age thirty, which the association has coordinated since 1977 in conjunction with the International Institute for Strategic Studies. A directory of the first seven years' participants in the New Faces series

was published by the association in 1983.

In the early 1980s, with the assistance of the Ford Foundation, ACA devoted an increasing proportion of its resources to secondary school and college-level educational projects. An illustrated primer covering fundamental concepts in arms control and national security—the product of meticulous writing and rigorous pilot testing—was scheduled to be published late in 1985. The association also launched a series of curriculum development and instructional programs with the convening of an unusual conference of social studies supervisors from forty-three states, cosponsored with the

*ACA President Herbert Scoville, Jr.*

*Discussants at Arms Control Association annual meeting: from left, Col. John G. Keliher (ret.), William H. Kincade, and John B. Rhinelander*

Consortium for International Studies Education (CISE). In the months following this conference, ACA and CISE staff gave frequent presentations on arms control and national security instruction to regional and national conferences of high school social studies teachers. Marie M. Hoguet, who joined ACA in 1984, served as its first education coordinator.

Upon taking over as executive director in 1985, Keeny, a former deputy director of the U.S. Arms Control and Disarmament Agency who came to the association from the National Academy of Sciences, where he had been scholar in residence, undertook a broad review of ACA's objectives for the latter half of the 1980s with the assistance of Jack W. Mendelsohn, who succeeded Julia A. Moore as deputy director.

Foremost among ACA priorities is a program of policy analysis, media outreach, and public education that addresses the long-term impact on nuclear strategy and the prospects for arms limitation of the development by the United States and the Soviet Union of space-based weapons and missile defense systems—familiarly known as "Star Wars." ACA initially directed its efforts toward countering the potential short-term threat to the ABM Treaty posed by these projected weapons developments. This program is closely followed on the ACA agenda by a similar effort aimed at illuminating the unique arms control challenges posed by new and projected offensive strategic weapons. ACA has sought to meet these program objectives both through its continuing support for the National Campaign to Save the ABM Treaty and through the preparation of detailed analyses of the key policy questions that have arisen in the course of these new nuclear debates.

*Strobe Talbott, of* Time *magazine, addresses Arms Control Association annual meeting*

The Face-to-Face program is a continuing forum for the intensive consideration of major international issues, jointly sponsored by the Endowment and the American Foreign Service Association. During the 1980s, Face-to-Face has come to occupy a premier position among Washing-

*Donald F. McHenry, ambassador to the United Nations in the Carter administration, leads a Face-to-Face discussion*

**Lt. Gen. Brent Scowcroft (ret.), national security adviser in the Ford administration and chairman of President Reagan's Commission on Strategic Forces, speaks at a Face-to-Face program. At left is Ronald A. Dwight, Face-to-Face director for 1984-85**

ton's numerous unofficial avenues for discussion of foreign policy.

Face-to-Face is directed each year by a Foreign Service officer on leave from the State Department, who is selected by the Endowment. The program consists of meetings over dinner at the Carnegie Conference Center. Each of the thirty to forty annual sessions features one or more guest speakers who address preselected topics drawn from the array of pressing international concerns. Guest speakers include current and former American officials and diplomats, foreign dignitaries visiting Washington, American and foreign political activists, business leaders, journalists, and specialists and scholars from around the world.

The program's skillfully assembled audiences are drawn from an extensive roster of prominent Americans—policymakers, area specialists, journalists, and private citizens—selected for their special expertise or interest in the topic slated for discussion.

By bringing together knowledgeable, diverse audiences with compelling speakers for extended "off-the-record" sessions, Face-to-Face facilitates an unusually candid and sophisticated interchange. Individuals who do not normally have the chance to gather under one roof are exposed to diverse viewpoints and useful professional contacts, and speakers are provided the opportunity to interact frankly with a small audience of particularly well-informed Americans.

**Recent Face-to-Face Directors**
Sharon Wilkinson, 1979-80
Robert J. Einhorn, 1980-81
Victor S. Gray, Jr., 1981-82
Mark L. Wiznitzer, 1982-83
Kenneth J. Dillon, 1983-84
Ronald A. Dwight, 1984-85
Yvonne F. Thayer, 1985-86

*K. Shankar Bajpai, Indian ambassador to the United States, a Face-to-Face speaker*

# FOREIGN POLICY

*L*aunched in 1970 with the purpose of contributing original perspectives and new voices to the dialogue on world affairs, *Foreign Policy* magazine, which is now owned and published by the Carnegie Endowment, was recognized from the outset as one of the most valuable and provocative sources of commentary on and analysis of international problems. Since 1980, under the editorship of Charles William Maynes, former assistant secretary of state for international organization affairs, *Foreign Policy* has grown significantly in circulation, has been formally recognized for outstanding coverage of nuclear arms issues, and has continued to distinguish itself in all international fields by publishing articles that have helped shape the agenda of the foreign affairs debate.

*Charles William Maynes*

**W**hite Americans seem to have divided into two camps—conservatives who are callous in their sense of resentment and superiority toward the Third World, and liberals who are cloying in their mood of meekness and guilt toward developing countries.

Charles William Maynes,
*Washington Post,*
September 18, 1983.

*Foreign Policy* is characterized by an ideologically diverse mix of topical and scholarly essays. In addition to featuring authoritative analyses of the world's key diplomatic problems, such as U.S.-Soviet relations and arms control, the magazine often investigates newer—and less scrutinized—international issues, such as the foreign-policy influence of media coverage, international resource and environmental management, and the psychological bases of the foreign-policy process.

Many *Foreign Policy* articles of recent years have received wide notice in public and official circles for raising the profile of emerging issues or examining familiar topics in a revealing manner. Stephen S. Rosenfeld's exploration of anti-Semitism and American foreign policy, Lester C. Thurow's study of the foreign-policy consequences of the American economic decline, and General George M. Seignious II and Jonathan Paul Yates's analysis of the unsettling impact on Western security of the nuclear modernization plans of France and the United Kingdom are prominent examples.

Other pieces have received considerable media coverage because of their unusual disclosures or their unique perspectives. Former U.S. Ambassador William H. Sullivan's recounting of events leading to the Iranian revolution supplied key elements to the historical record of that period. In a landmark article, "Green Light, Lebanon," Ze'ev Schiff exposed the American role in the fateful Israeli decision to invade Lebanon in 1982. Lloyd N. Cutler, a former presidential counsel, offered a revealing "insider's" account of the damaging effects of the Carter administration's attempt to take television news coverage into account in its policy deliberations. Wayne S. Smith, for many years the State Department's top Cuba expert, explored the contradictions and false steps in the Cuba policies of successive American administrations.

*L. Maxine Fowler, fulfillment manager of* Foreign Policy, *left, and, above, Peggy Jarvis, circulation director*

Several recent *Foreign Policy* articles have come to be considered essential reading among foreign-policymakers and students of international relations. In an essay that remains an important and controversial point of departure in the strategic debate, "Under the Nuclear Gun: Victory Is Possible," Colin S. Gray and Keith Payne argued that the United States ought to prepare to fight and win a potential nuclear conflict. Early in the Reagan administration C. Fred Bergsten warned that "The Costs of Reaganomics" would be found in a rapidly growing foreign trade imbalance. Lawrence T. Caldwell and Robert Legvold's sobering assessment of Soviet perceptions, "Reagan through Soviet Eyes," is often cited for its contribution to an understanding of recent U.S.-Soviet relations.

Deputy Assistant Secretary of Defense Nestor D. Sanchez's elaboration of the hard-line view of U.S. stakes in Central America, "The Communist Threat," served to catalyze the domestic policy debate. Also widely discussed were Fouad Ajami's ambitious Middle East survey, "The Bigger Picture: The Arab Road"; Assistant Secretary of State James L. Malone's rationale for American rejection of the Law-of-the-Sea Treaty, "Who Needs the Sea Treaty?"; and Robert S. Leiken's illuminating study of the Soviet bloc's quiet yet resolute pursuit of influence in the Western Hemisphere, "Eastern Winds in Latin America."

Since the late 1970s, *Foreign Policy* has sponsored a series of breakfast press conferences in the Endowment's Washington conference center. Speakers have been drawn from the ranks of visiting foreign officials and dignitaries, prominent members of the Washington foreign-policy community, and Americans returning from trips abroad. In addition to providing a congenial forum for the discussion of major current developments, the press breakfasts have routinely offered the

Foreign Policy *Copy Editor* *Joan D. Berne*

Washington press corps a valuable source of background information on a wide range of major international issues.

Guest speakers in recent years have included such figures as former Australian Prime Minister Malcolm Fraser; Prince Norodom Sihanouk of Cambodia; former U.S. Ambassador to the United Nations Donald F. McHenry; Iraqi Foreign Minister Tariq Aziz; Jordanian Foreign Minister Taher N. Masri; Petra Kelly, a leading West German peace activist; Jacques Chirac, the mayor of Paris; Guillermo Ungo, president of the Democratic Revolutionary Front of El Salvador; Adolfo Calero, president of the national directorate of the anti-Sandinista Nicaraguan Democratic Force; South African Bishop Desmond Tutu; and West German Chancellor Helmut Kohl.

In addition to his editorial responsibilities, Maynes has been a frequent contributor of articles on international relations to major newspapers and periodicals in the United States. His columns appear regularly in the *Los Angeles Times,* and his writings are distributed to numerous papers by the *New York Times* syndication service. Maynes is often called upon to serve as a foreign affairs commentator on television and radio broadcasts in the United States and abroad. Associate Editor Alan Tonelson, who succeeded Leigh Bruce in 1983, has also contributed articles and book reviews on foreign affairs to leading American newspapers and periodicals.

*Foreign Policy's* quarterly publishing endeavors have been complemented during the past few years by the publication of two special essay collections and by the production of a popular foreign relations calendar. In 1980 the magazine published *A Decade of Foreign Policy,* a volume of important articles drawn from its first ten years. In 1983, in conjunction with Westview Press, *Foreign Policy* collected under one cover many of the pieces on Latin America that it had published since its inception.

*Associate Editor Alan Tonelson with* Foreign Policy *interns*

## Speakers at the Carnegie Endowment, 1980-85*

David Aaron
Elliott Abrams
J. Adonis
Albert Aghazarian
Susanna Agnelli
Ahmad Rithauddeen bin Ismail
Erdil K. Akay
Warren Allmand
Enrique Alvarez Córdova
Desaix Anderson
Fernando Andrade Díaz-Durán
Franz Andriessen
Hannes Androsch
Julio Cesar Araoz
Georgi Arbatov
Moshe Arens
Alvaro Arguello Hurtado
Roberto Arguello Hurtado
Obed Y. Asamoah
Les Aspin
Tariq Aziz
William B. Bader
K. Shankar Bajpai
Michael D. Barnes
Gert Bastian
Adolfo Battaglia
Osama el Baz
Robin L. Beard
Marie-Luise Beck-Oberdorf
Peter Bell
Meron Benvenisti
Douglas Bereuter
Eivinn Berg
Raoul Berger
C. Fred Bergsten
Georges Berthoin
Joseph R. Biden
Kurt H. Biedenkopf
Jeff Bingaman
Barry M. Blechman
Hans Blix
Alfons Böcker
Gerard Bolla
Bernard Bot
Rodrigo Botero
Mohamed Boucetta
Willy Brandt
John B. Breaux
Zbigniew Brzezinski
Richard R. Burt
Goler Butcher
Alfred Cahen

Adolfo Calero
James Callaghan
Bernt Carlsson
Peter Carrington
Juan Manuel Casella
Robert Cassen
Fabio Castillo Figueroa
Jaime Castillo Velasco
Alfredo César
Bernard Chidzero
Henk Chin-a-sen
Edmund O. Z. Chipamaunga
Jacques Chirac
Charles Clements
William E. Colby
Emilio Colombo
José Concepción
John K. Cooley
Chester L. Cooper
Richard N. Cooper
Baltasar Corrada Del Río
Jean-Pierre Cot
Theodore Couloumbis
Chester A. Crocker
Arturo José Cruz
Lloyd N. Cutler
Walter L. Cutler
Thomas d'Aquino
George Daniel
Pieter Dankert
Jacques de Groote
Roland de Kergolay
Luigi Ciriaco De Mita
John de St. Jorre
Jonathan Dean
Jean-François Deniau
Roy Denman
Edward J. Derwinski
James B. Devine
Giuseppe Di Gennaro
Eberhard Diepgen
A. R. Shams-ud Doha
Sean Donlon
Hedley Donovan
Morris Draper
Marne A. Dubs
Barrie Dunsmore
Hugh Dykes
Lawrence S. Eagleburger
Roger Edde
Horst Ehmke
Warren Eisenberg

Robert Eisner
Jack Elder
Sukru Elekdag
Fernando Eleta
Theodore L. Eliot, Jr.
Thomas O. Enders
Paul Engo
Magda Enriquez
Erhard Eppler
Stephen van Evera
Larry L. Fabian
Mansour Farhang
Dante Fascell
Omar I. el Fathaly
Geza Feketekuty
Mariano Fiallos Oyanguren
Garret FitzGerald
Lisa Fitzgerald
Thomas S. Foley
Bernardus G. Fourie
Wyche Fowler
Douglas A. Fraser
Malcolm Fraser
Orville Freeman
Elias Freij
Knut Frydenlung
Alton Frye
Lawrence H. Fuchs
Jama Mohamed Galib
Richard Gardner
Monique Garnier-Lançon
Patrick Gautrat
Leslie H. Gelb
Jean-Louis Gergorin
Robert K. German
Brian Germond
Alexis Ghalanos
Chris Giannou
Joseph A. Gilbert
Richard Gilmore
Ian Gilmour
Hans-Joachim Gläsner
John Glenn
Robert F. Goheen
Nahum Goldmann
Leonel Gómez
Alvaro Gómez Hurtado
Eric Gonsalves
Edward Gonzalez
Albert Gore, Jr.
Xavier Gorostiaga
Allan E. Gotlieb

Alexander Gowrie
Daniel Graham
William H. Gray III
Diego Ramiro Guelar
Mustafa Gursel
Hildegard Hamm-Brücher
Selig S. Harrison
Gary Hart
Arthur Hartman
J. Bryan Hehir
Curt Heidenreich
Claude Hemmer
Nicholas Henderson
Peter Hermes
Rafael Hernández-Colón
Martin J. Hillenbrand
Deane Hinton
John H. Holdridge
Johan Jorgen Holst
Robert D. Hormats
David Howell
John Hume
Robert Hunter
Sayed Hussein Husseini
William G. Hyland
Yurchi Ichikawa
Bobby R. Inman
Andrew J. Jacovides
Idriss Jazairy
Josef Joffe
Willard Johnson
James Jonah
Brennon Jones
David C. Jones
Karl Kaiser
Max M. Kampelman
Nancy Kassebaum
Petra Kelly
Rashid Khalidi
Walid Khalidi
Kim Dae Jung
Kim Kyung-Won
William H. Kincade
Neal Kinnock
Ismat Kittani
Helmut Kohl
Volkmar Köhler
Robert W. Komer
Ken Kramer
Martha Krämer
Robert H. Kupperman
Akira Kuroyanagi
Bernard Lewis
Robert J. Lieber
Sol M. Linowitz
Jan M. Lodal

Eduard Lohse
Sriniwas L. Lokre
José da Silva Lopes
Winston Lord
Rüdiger Löwe
Jan Hendrik Lubbers
Princeton Lyman
John McAward
Robert J. McCloskey
Harold McCusker
Donald F. McHenry
David MacMichael
Manon Maren-Griesebach
Claudio Martelli
Joao Filipe Martins
Tahir Nash'at ul-Masri
Nawaf Massalha
Leonardo Mathias
Jack F. Matlock
Christopher Mayhew
Charles William Maynes
Roman Mayorga Quiros
Amadou Mahtar M'Bow
Rigoberta Menchu
Andre Mernier
Alois Mertes
Marshall Meyer
Benjamin Mkapa
Alois Mock
Luis Alberto Monge
Powell A. Moore
Thomas Morony
Raphael Mothe
Stanley Motjuwadi
Dirk F. Mudge
Andrew Mulligan
John Naisbitt
K.R. Narayanan
Nguza Karl-I-Bond
Matthew Nimetz
William A. Niskanen
Paul Nitze
William D. Nordhaus
Joseph S. Nye
Robert B. Oakley
Philip A. Odeen
George Odlum
Daniel Oduber
Saburo Okita
Lionel H. Olmer
Ehud Olmert
Robert G. O'Neill
David Owen
Robert Oxnam
Yves Pagniez
Michael Palliser

* People on this list were the featured speakers at Face-to-Face programs, *Foreign Policy* magazine press breakfasts, Mid-Atlantic Club luncheons and semi-annual Endowment trustees meetings.

*From left, Alton Frye, Washington director of the Council on Foreign Relations; C. Fred Bergsten, director of the Institute for International Economics; and Frank E. Loy, president of the German Marshall Fund of the United States. All three organizations are located with the Carnegie Endowment at 11 Dupont Circle in Washington*

*Office Manager Rosemary Gwynn, below, and, right, Accountant Lori A. Mennella with Michael V. O'Hare, director of Finance and Administration*

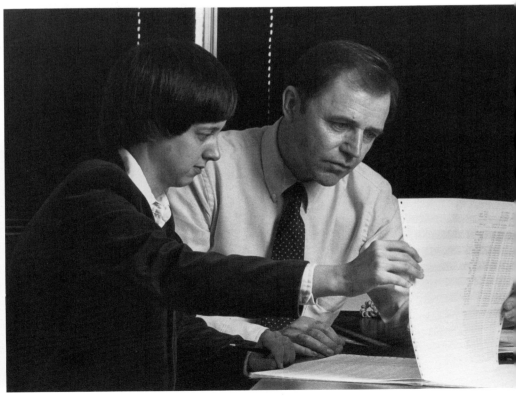

68

## Finance and Administration

Michael V. O'Hare, *Director*
Karen G. Roberts, *Personnel Coordinator*
Lori A. Mennella, *Accountant*
Rosemary Gwynn, *Office Manager*
Gregory D. Redmon, *Conference Center Coordinator*
John P. Gwynn
Willie E. Holloman
Renée M. Key
Dianne J. Lerner
Rudolph C. Noble
Richard C. Tardy
Lynde Tracey

## Project Staff

Maria Luz Alvarez-Wilson
Virginia T. Babin
Amanda S. Cadle
Mary J. Child
Kathleen M. Defty
Anne K. Gibbs
Sara J. Goodgame
Violet Lee
Mary Elizabeth Lightowler
Charlene Morrison
Geoff Peck
Julie A. Reed
Jane S. Ross
Alease M. Vaughn
David Weiner
Catherine Yost

## Library

Jane E. Lowenthal, *Librarian*
Jenny C. Grimsley
Monica M. Yin

*Jane E. Lowenthal and Jack Shepherd at the Library of Congress*

# Current Guidelines

## I. Purpose

The activities of the Endowment are shaped by its charter to advance the cause of world peace. It seeks to be relevant by focusing on critical topics of American and international policy with a changing mix of projects conducted by experienced people. It achieves effectiveness by serving as a forum for discussion and debate and as a center for analysis and education about the issues and events threatening world peace. The Endowment's operating objectives are to analyze, to inform, and to influence debate and policy formulation on the central issues of the day.

## II. Senior and Resident Associates

To fulfill those objectives, the Endowment seeks talented and experienced people from a wide variety of backgrounds to bring their knowledge and experience to bear for differing periods of time on pressing issues of the day. The selection of these Associates depends normally on the nature of the issue: in one instance, the ability to analyze, to bring knowledge and experience to bear on a novel issue may be most important; in another, the bringing together of diverse viewpoints to illuminate the issues or to find a middle ground may be most appropriate. Above all, integrity, judgment, and independence of thought guide the Endowment's selections.

## III. The Environment

Critical to the Endowment's success is the environment in which its staff works. That environment must be conducive to independent inquiry and freedom of expression, and marked by respect for differing viewpoints and fresh thought. Accordingly, the Endowment seeks to provide a hospitable but neutral umbrella under which responsible analysis and debate may be civilly conducted, encouraging its Associates to write and speak freely on the subjects of their work. The Endowment normally does not take positions or make endorsements or recommendations. Consistent with its dedication to independence of thought and freedom of expression, the Endowment funds its activities primarily from its own resources, occasionally supplemented by other non-governmental, philanthropic sources of support.

*Board of Trustees*

*The top floor of this building on Dupont Circle is the headquarters of the Carnegie Endowment, and its conference center is on the floor below*

DESIGN: SCHUM & STOBER, GRAPHIC DESIGN, INC.
PHOTOGRAPHS BY CHAD EVANS WYATT